One-Minute Math

Developmental Drill

Level A Multiplication
Factors 0 to 5

Grades 2-3

Author: Theresa Warnick
Cover Artist: Good Neighbor Press

Frank Schaffer Publications®

Send all inquiries to:
Frank Schaffer Publications
8720 Orion Place
Columbus, Ohio 43240-2111

ISBN 0-7647-0395-1

8 9 10 11 PAT 12 11 10 09

DIRECTIONS FOR USE

Setting up the Program

Reproduce enough copies of the tests for the class. You may wish to separate the tests by fact into file folders and organize the folders in a storage box. This provides handy access to the tests and a quick view of the pages which need to be replenished.

Using a manila file folder for each student offers easy organization and provides a simple method of distributing the daily tests.

Using the Flash Cards

A set of flash cards is required for each student. These serve as additional facilitators in learning and retaining basic math facts.

When beginning the program, give each student only those facts he or she has mastered on the progress chart and the first unchecked fact. This card will correspond to the test the student will be taking. Each time another fact is mastered, give the student the card for the next fact. When starting at the Zero Rule, the student should be given all the zero flash cards. You may wish to present this rule as: zero times any factor equals zero. When the student progresses to the One Rule, the student is given all the one times flash cards. The One Rule may be presented as: one times any factor equals that factor. Unmastered flash cards may be left in the student's folder for easy access.

Encourage the use of the flash cards at home as well as at school. Depending on the number of cards being reviewed, you may wish to spend five to fifteen minutes a day on flash card practice.

Using the Bulletin Board

The "Math Facts Are Hot Stuff" bulletin board theme can be used to highlight the multiplication facts on which each student is working. Using the reproducible art found on pages vi-vii write the math facts on the cactus, kangaroo rat, pottery and roadrunner. You may enlarge the reproducible illustrations for the bulletin board by using the opaque projector or make a transparency of the illustrations in order to use the overhead projector.

Using the Progress Charts

The progress chart shows the multiplication facts and indicates the scope and sequence of Level A (factors zero to five). By checking off each fact a student masters, you can record each student's progress. Each student may track his or her own progress by coloring a copy of the personal progress chart found in the reproducible pages.

The Letter to Parents

The letter provided will help make parents aware of the objectives, components and methods of the **One-Minute Math Developmental Drill** series.

Awards and Certificate of Achievement

When a student completes a designated number of facts, you may wish to present him or her with an award found in the reproducible pages. The certificate may be used when all of the facts in the Level A Multiplication are mastered.

Using the Manipulative Mats

It is important that students develop a good understanding of numbers. The following activities will help students create relations for numbers and will help strengthen their number sense.

Have the students work with a variety of materials on the manipulative mat (page viii). These mats may be laminated for extended use.

1. Select a number of counters representing products for factors zero to five. If, for example, the selected factors are four times five, the student may separate the counters on the mat into four groups of five counters. Next, the student should verbalize the parts shown, for example: "Four times five equals twenty." Allow the students adequate practice in manipulating the counters into sets for other factor combinations. (See illustration A.)

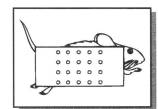

2. Students should continue working with their manipulative mats and counters. On copies of activity page ix, have the students draw the factors for a selected product and write its corresponding multiplication sentence. (See illustration B.)

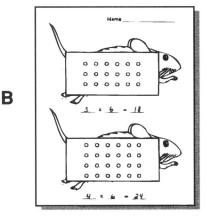

3. Select a product and ask the students to place the correct number of counters on their mats. Have the students write that number at the top of a blank sheet of paper. Students should use their counters to find all the possible combinations of factors for the product and then record the multiplication sentences.

4. Have the students work with partners. Select a product for factors zero to five. One student should place the counters on the mat to show the multiplication set (e.g., 3 x 4) and cover one side of the mat. In the example, if the product is known to be twelve, the student's partner must answer the question, "Four times what number makes twelve?" Continue this activity with other products. (See illustration C.)

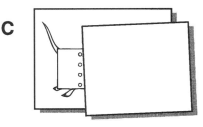

Using the Game Sheets

Game Sheets (pages x-xi): Fill in the blank spaces on the path with the number facts you wish to reinforce. Some students may be interested in decorating the game sheet with markers or color crayons and giving the game a title. Each game sheet may be laminated for extended use. Using a gameboard spinner, the student moves ahead the number of spaces shown and must correctly answer the number fact to remain on that space. If the correct answer is given, the next player may take a turn. If the student answers incorrectly, he or she returns to the previously held space.

Large Game Sheet (pages xii-xiii): Attach page A to page B. This large game sheet may be laminated for extended use. When playing the game, a student advances the game piece by dropping a marker (coin, button, etc.) onto the center of the playing board. (If the marker does not land on any fact, the student forfeits his or her turn.) The student must answer the math fact or facts the marker is touching and may move the game piece ahead the number of correct answers given. For example: If the marker is touching two facts and the student answers only one correctly, the student may advance the game piece one space.

Each game may end when one player reaches the final space on the path or continues until all players reach the end space. Students may also play in teams.

Using the Timed Tests

Level A Multiplication teaches factors zero to five. Each sheet contains 30 problems. There is a pretest and posttest for placement and evaluation. The particular fact the student is learning appears 40% of the time (twelve problems) on each test. The last previous fact mastered occurs 10% to 20% of the time (three to six problems). The remaining 40% to 50% of the problems on each sheet are those previously learned by the student, except for those pages labeled as tests, which usually present each fact only once. Each sequence of facts, such as the "multiples of two, " ends with a test just focusing on those facts. This test can be used as a diagnostic tool to pinpoint particular sequences of facts not known. For instance, a student may already know the "multiples of three," but not know the "multiples of four." These section tests may help to asses this. Students using the program should also take these tests when appropriate.

Each student should complete a timed test every day if possible, starting with the lowest fact on the progress chart for that student. Remind the students to note the fact written in the upper lefthand corner, which indicates the fact on which they are working. Students must complete all the problems on a sheet accurately **in one minute** before advancing to the next fact. If the student has not completely and accurately answered all the problems when the minute has elapsed, he or she must complete a test for the same fact the next day. If students have extreme difficulty passing each fact page, you may wish to lengthen the amount of time allowed to complete the page by five or ten seconds.

It is important to allow students to see their progress on the same fact. All attempted tests may be left in the folder and the same fact test added on top for the next day. Students will become more proficient each time they are retested on the same fact until they finally master it.

Not all students will complete the entire program, but they will possess a greater proficiency of the facts they have mastered. Mastery, rather than completion, is the goal of the program.

Dear Parent,

In order to develop a good mathematics foundation, it is important that your child learn basic multiplication and division facts. The **One-Minute Math Developmental Drill** program enables children to achieve this goal. The idea behind this program is that children must master a particular math fact before they are introduced to a new fact.

A flash card will be sent home each time your child begins learning a new multiplication fact. The flash cards will help your child memorize these facts more readily. Please have your child practice daily with all of the flash cards you have received. He or she should work toward answering each card in less than two seconds. Help your child with this activity if possible. Since it may take several days to commit some facts to memory, be patient with your child. Children will not learn all facts at the same rate. Do not expect your child to bring home a new flash card every day.

The Level A Multiplication program includes:

1. Pretest and posttest for placement and evaluation

2. 42 individual fact tests on factors zero to five

    a. Each test contains 30 problems

    b. The particular fact a student is learning is covered in 40% of the test

    c. The previously learned fact is covered in 10% to 20% of the test

3. 57 flash cards for practicing the selected facts

4. Certificate upon completion

Thank you for working with me on this program.
Please contact me if you have any questions or concerns.

Sincerely,

Reproducible Art

Reproducible Art

FS-23245 One-Minute Math Level A Multiplication

Manipulative Mat

FS-23245 One-Minute Math Level A Multiplication

Activity Page

Name _____

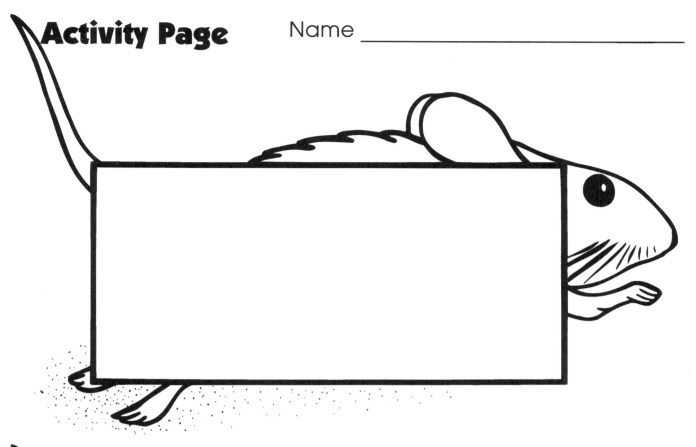

_____ x _____ = _____

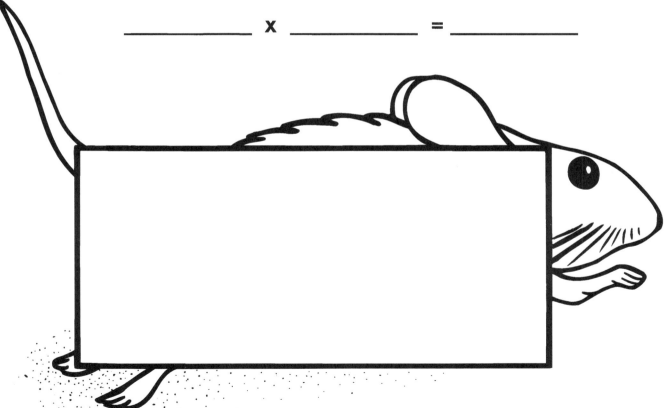

_____ x _____ = _____

ix

Game Sheet

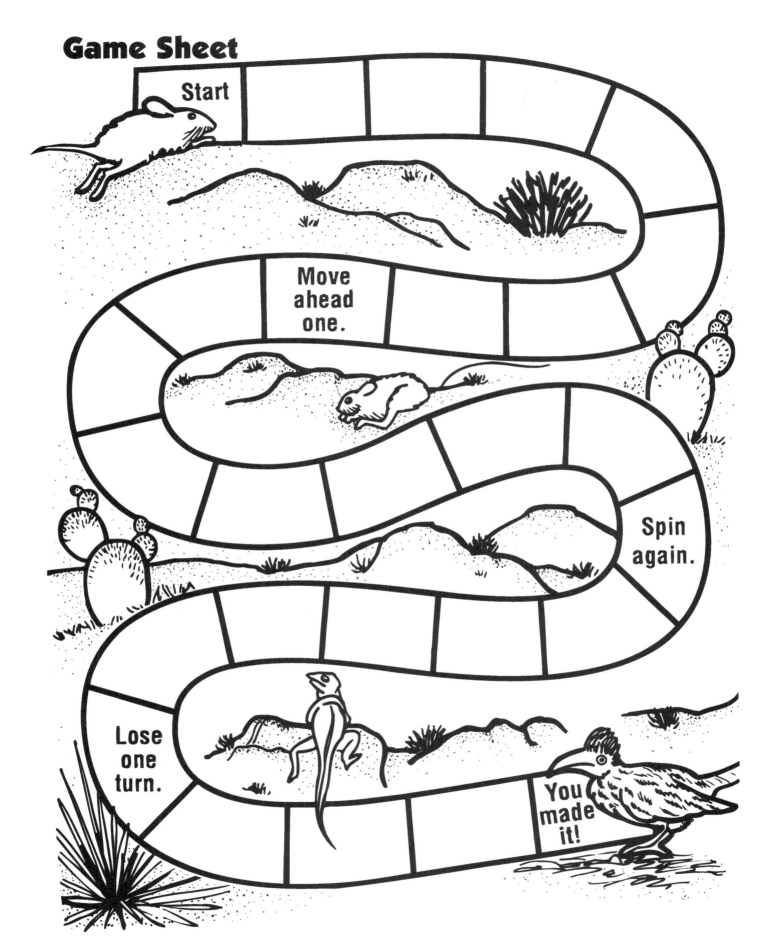

Start

Move ahead one.

Spin again.

Lose one turn.

You made it!

X

FS-23245 One-Minute Math Level A Multiplication

Game Sheet

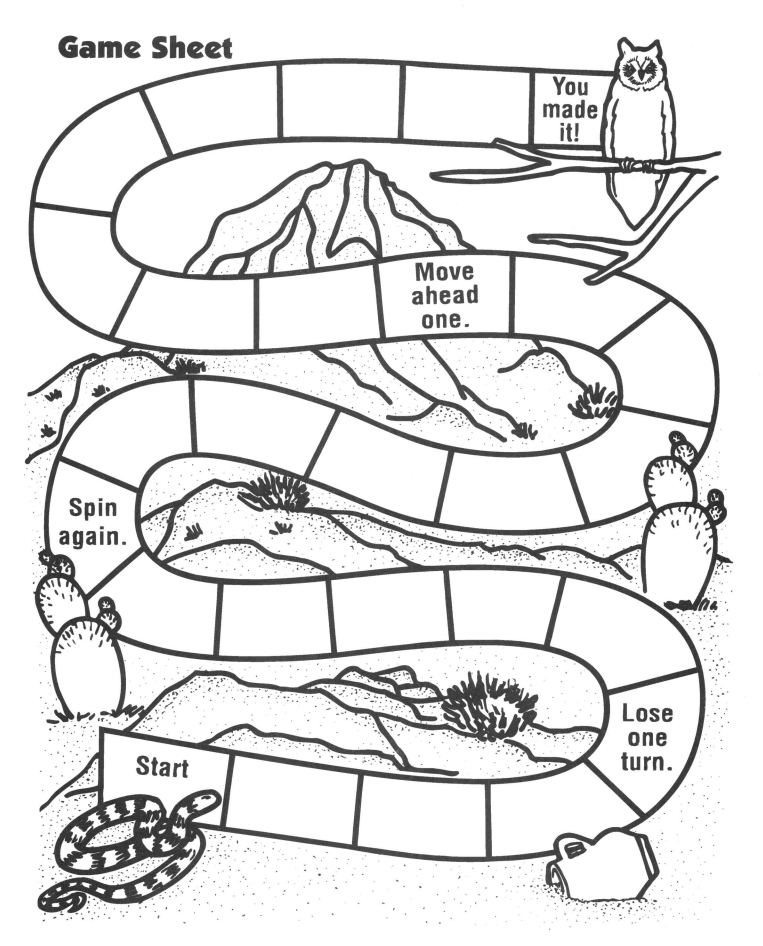

You made it!

Move ahead one.

Spin again.

Lose one turn.

Start

Game Sheet

Start

Finish

You did it!

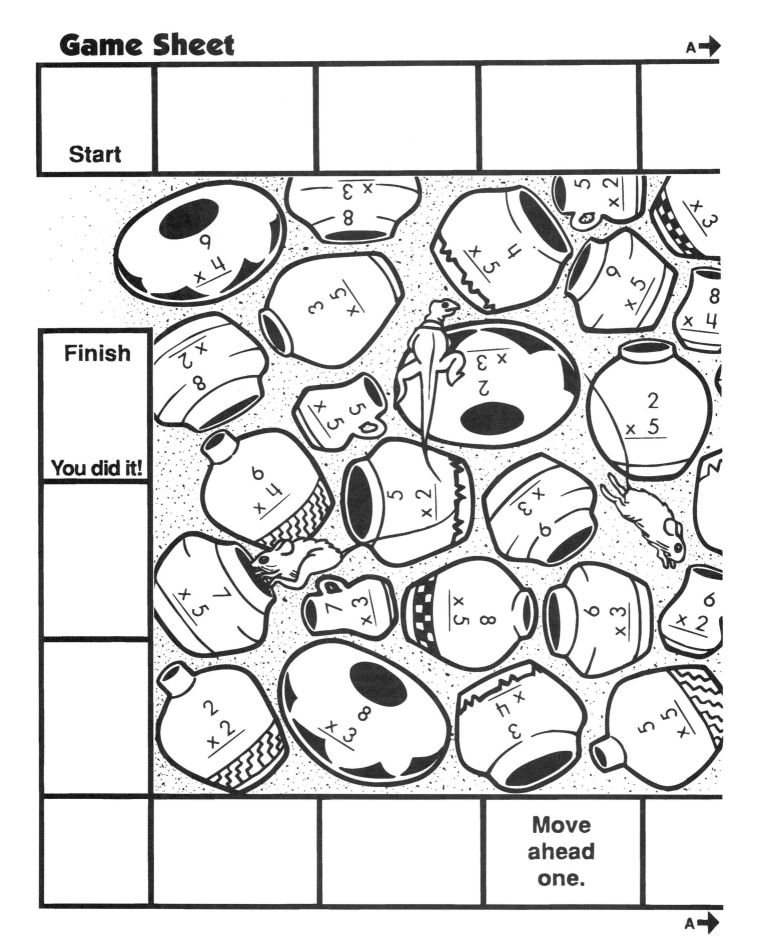

Move ahead one.

xii FS-23245 One-Minute Math Level A Multiplication

FS-23245 One-Minute Math Level A Multiplication

Awards and Certificate

I'm Racing

For Facts!

I Know
My Facts!

Congratulations!

_____

has completed Level A Multiplication
Factors 0 to 5

TERRIFIC JOB!

Name	Pre-test	0 Rule	1 Rule	2 x 2	3 x 2	4 x 2	5 x 2	6 x 2	7 x 2	8 x 2	9 x 2	10 x 2	2's Test	2 x 3	3 x 3	4 x 3	5 x 3	6 x 3	7 x 3	8 x 3	9 x 3	10 x 3	3's Test

Progress Chart
Level A Multiplication   Factors 0 to 5

Name	2 x 4	3 x 4	4 x 4	5 x 4	6 x 4	7 x 4	8 x 4	9 x 4	10 x 4	4's Test	2 x 5	3 x 5	4 x 5	5 x 5	6 x 5	7 x 5	8 x 5	9 x 5	10 x 5	5's Test	Test

       FS-23245 One-Minute Math Level A Multiplication

Student Progress Chart

This chart belongs to

Color each math fact you have learned.

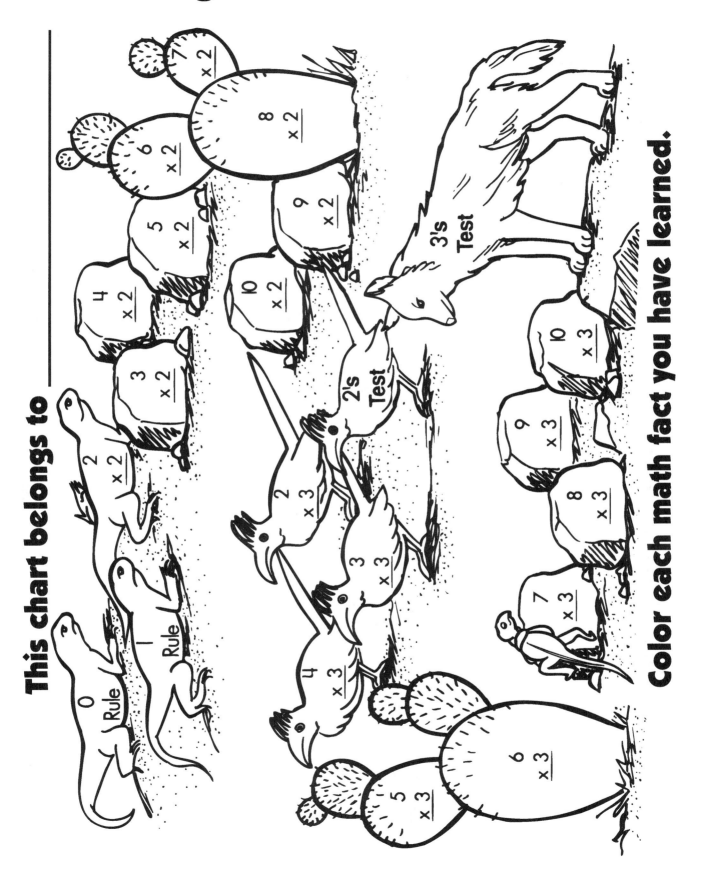

0 Rule

1 Rule

$\begin{array}{r} 2 \\ \times 2 \\ \hline \end{array}$

$\begin{array}{r} 3 \\ \times 2 \\ \hline \end{array}$

$\begin{array}{r} 4 \\ \times 2 \\ \hline \end{array}$

$\begin{array}{r} 5 \\ \times 2 \\ \hline \end{array}$

$\begin{array}{r} 6 \\ \times 2 \\ \hline \end{array}$

$\begin{array}{r} 7 \\ \times 2 \\ \hline \end{array}$

$\begin{array}{r} 8 \\ \times 2 \\ \hline \end{array}$

$\begin{array}{r} 9 \\ \times 2 \\ \hline \end{array}$

$\begin{array}{r} 10 \\ \times 2 \\ \hline \end{array}$

2's Test

3's Test

$\begin{array}{r} 2 \\ \times 3 \\ \hline \end{array}$

$\begin{array}{r} 3 \\ \times 3 \\ \hline \end{array}$

$\begin{array}{r} 4 \\ \times 3 \\ \hline \end{array}$

$\begin{array}{r} 5 \\ \times 3 \\ \hline \end{array}$

$\begin{array}{r} 6 \\ \times 3 \\ \hline \end{array}$

$\begin{array}{r} 7 \\ \times 3 \\ \hline \end{array}$

$\begin{array}{r} 8 \\ \times 3 \\ \hline \end{array}$

$\begin{array}{r} 9 \\ \times 3 \\ \hline \end{array}$

$\begin{array}{r} 10 \\ \times 3 \\ \hline \end{array}$

FS-23245 One-Minute Math Level A Multiplication

Student Progress Chart

This chart belongs to _____

Color each math fact you have learned.

Level A Pretest   Name _____

5 × 2	7 × 4	10 × 2	8 × 5	7 × 2
10 × 4	3 × 7	5 × 5	2 × 4	4 × 8
2 × 8	5 × 9	10 × 3	8 × 3	4 × 4
3 × 5	9 × 1	9 × 4	6 × 3	7 × 5
7 × 0	5 × 6	3 × 3	9 × 2	6 × 4
4 × 5	9 × 3	6 × 2	10 × 5	4 × 3

Level A 0-Rule   Name _____

$$\begin{array}{r} 0 \\ \times\ 1 \\ \hline \end{array} \qquad \begin{array}{r} 8 \\ \times\ 0 \\ \hline \end{array} \qquad \begin{array}{r} 0 \\ \times\ 3 \\ \hline \end{array} \qquad \begin{array}{r} 6 \\ \times\ 0 \\ \hline \end{array} \qquad \begin{array}{r} 0 \\ \times\ 9 \\ \hline \end{array}$$

$$\begin{array}{r} 3 \\ \times\ 0 \\ \hline \end{array} \qquad \begin{array}{r} 0 \\ \times\ 5 \\ \hline \end{array} \qquad \begin{array}{r} 2 \\ \times\ 0 \\ \hline \end{array} \qquad \begin{array}{r} 0 \\ \times\ 4 \\ \hline \end{array} \qquad \begin{array}{r} 0 \\ \times\ 10 \\ \hline \end{array}$$

$$\begin{array}{r} 0 \\ \times\ 8 \\ \hline \end{array} \qquad \begin{array}{r} 7 \\ \times\ 0 \\ \hline \end{array} \qquad \begin{array}{r} 0 \\ \times\ 0 \\ \hline \end{array} \qquad \begin{array}{r} 2 \\ \times\ 0 \\ \hline \end{array} \qquad \begin{array}{r} 0 \\ \times\ 6 \\ \hline \end{array}$$

$$\begin{array}{r} 5 \\ \times\ 0 \\ \hline \end{array} \qquad \begin{array}{r} 0 \\ \times\ 9 \\ \hline \end{array} \qquad \begin{array}{r} 10 \\ \times\ 0 \\ \hline \end{array} \qquad \begin{array}{r} 4 \\ \times\ 0 \\ \hline \end{array} \qquad \begin{array}{r} 0 \\ \times\ 3 \\ \hline \end{array}$$

$$\begin{array}{r} 7 \\ \times\ 0 \\ \hline \end{array} \qquad \begin{array}{r} 1 \\ \times\ 0 \\ \hline \end{array} \qquad \begin{array}{r} 0 \\ \times\ 6 \\ \hline \end{array} \qquad \begin{array}{r} 0 \\ \times\ 8 \\ \hline \end{array} \qquad \begin{array}{r} 5 \\ \times\ 0 \\ \hline \end{array}$$

$$\begin{array}{r} 9 \\ \times\ 0 \\ \hline \end{array} \qquad \begin{array}{r} 0 \\ \times\ 2 \\ \hline \end{array} \qquad \begin{array}{r} 4 \\ \times\ 0 \\ \hline \end{array} \qquad \begin{array}{r} 0 \\ \times\ 7 \\ \hline \end{array} \qquad \begin{array}{r} 0 \\ \times\ 0 \\ \hline \end{array}$$

                   FS-23245 One-Minute Math Level A Multiplication

Name _____

3 × 1	1 × 9	7 × 1	1 × 2	1 × 5
1 × 8	10 × 1	0 × 8	4 × 1	3 × 0
0 × 2	1 × 1	5 × 0	1 × 3	9 × 1
1 × 6	7 × 0	8 × 1	0 × 9	1 × 7
0 × 4	5 × 1	1 × 10	2 × 1	1 × 4
1 × 7	0 × 6	1 × 1	1 × 8	6 × 1

0 x 3	10 x 1	2 x 2	1 x 5	2 x 2
1 x 4	2 x 2	6 x 0	2 x 2	1 x 7
2 x 2	1 x 3	2 x 2	0 x 5	2 x 1
1 x 1	2 x 2	0 x 1	1 x 9	2 x 2
2 x 2	5 x 1	2 x 2	4 x 1	2 x 0
8 x 1	2 x 2	4 x 0	2 x 2	6 x 1

Level A 2 x 3   Name _____

2 x 2	7 x 1	3 x 2	8 x 0	2 x 3
1 x 1	2 x 3	0 x 0	3 x 2	2 x 2
3 x 2	2 x 2	2 x 3	1 x 4	9 x 1
10 x 0	2 x 3	2 x 2	1 x 6	3 x 2
2 x 3	1 x 2	3 x 2	0 x 7	2 x 2
2 x 2	3 x 2	1 x 8	2 x 3	9 x 0

$$
\begin{array}{r} 3 \\ \times\ 2 \\ \hline \end{array}
\qquad
\begin{array}{r} 0 \\ \times\ 5 \\ \hline \end{array}
\qquad
\begin{array}{r} 4 \\ \times\ 2 \\ \hline \end{array}
\qquad
\begin{array}{r} 2 \\ \times\ 2 \\ \hline \end{array}
\qquad
\begin{array}{r} 2 \\ \times\ 4 \\ \hline \end{array}
$$

$$
\begin{array}{r} 2 \\ \times\ 2 \\ \hline \end{array}
\qquad
\begin{array}{r} 2 \\ \times\ 4 \\ \hline \end{array}
\qquad
\begin{array}{r} 1 \\ \times\ 3 \\ \hline \end{array}
\qquad
\begin{array}{r} 4 \\ \times\ 2 \\ \hline \end{array}
\qquad
\begin{array}{r} 2 \\ \times\ 3 \\ \hline \end{array}
$$

$$
\begin{array}{r} 4 \\ \times\ 2 \\ \hline \end{array}
\qquad
\begin{array}{r} 3 \\ \times\ 2 \\ \hline \end{array}
\qquad
\begin{array}{r} 2 \\ \times\ 4 \\ \hline \end{array}
\qquad
\begin{array}{r} 6 \\ \times\ 0 \\ \hline \end{array}
\qquad
\begin{array}{r} 2 \\ \times\ 2 \\ \hline \end{array}
$$

$$
\begin{array}{r} 0 \\ \times\ 2 \\ \hline \end{array}
\qquad
\begin{array}{r} 2 \\ \times\ 4 \\ \hline \end{array}
\qquad
\begin{array}{r} 2 \\ \times\ 3 \\ \hline \end{array}
\qquad
\begin{array}{r} 8 \\ \times\ 1 \\ \hline \end{array}
\qquad
\begin{array}{r} 4 \\ \times\ 2 \\ \hline \end{array}
$$

$$
\begin{array}{r} 4 \\ \times\ 2 \\ \hline \end{array}
\qquad
\begin{array}{r} 2 \\ \times\ 2 \\ \hline \end{array}
\qquad
\begin{array}{r} 2 \\ \times\ 4 \\ \hline \end{array}
\qquad
\begin{array}{r} 10 \\ \times\ 1 \\ \hline \end{array}
\qquad
\begin{array}{r} 3 \\ \times\ 2 \\ \hline \end{array}
$$

$$
\begin{array}{r} 3 \\ \times\ 2 \\ \hline \end{array}
\qquad
\begin{array}{r} 2 \\ \times\ 4 \\ \hline \end{array}
\qquad
\begin{array}{r} 5 \\ \times\ 1 \\ \hline \end{array}
\qquad
\begin{array}{r} 4 \\ \times\ 2 \\ \hline \end{array}
\qquad
\begin{array}{r} 2 \\ \times\ 2 \\ \hline \end{array}
$$

$$
\begin{array}{r} 4 \\ \times\ 2 \\ \hline \end{array}
\qquad
\begin{array}{r} 2 \\ \times\ 2 \\ \hline \end{array}
\qquad
\begin{array}{r} 2 \\ \times\ 5 \\ \hline \end{array}
\qquad
\begin{array}{r} 3 \\ \times\ 2 \\ \hline \end{array}
\qquad
\begin{array}{r} 5 \\ \times\ 2 \\ \hline \end{array}
$$

$$
\begin{array}{r} 2 \\ \times\ 2 \\ \hline \end{array}
\qquad
\begin{array}{r} 5 \\ \times\ 2 \\ \hline \end{array}
\qquad
\begin{array}{r} 9 \\ \times\ 1 \\ \hline \end{array}
\qquad
\begin{array}{r} 2 \\ \times\ 5 \\ \hline \end{array}
\qquad
\begin{array}{r} 2 \\ \times\ 4 \\ \hline \end{array}
$$

$$
\begin{array}{r} 2 \\ \times\ 5 \\ \hline \end{array}
\qquad
\begin{array}{r} 4 \\ \times\ 2 \\ \hline \end{array}
\qquad
\begin{array}{r} 5 \\ \times\ 2 \\ \hline \end{array}
\qquad
\begin{array}{r} 0 \\ \times\ 4 \\ \hline \end{array}
\qquad
\begin{array}{r} 2 \\ \times\ 3 \\ \hline \end{array}
$$

$$
\begin{array}{r} 1 \\ \times\ 6 \\ \hline \end{array}
\qquad
\begin{array}{r} 5 \\ \times\ 2 \\ \hline \end{array}
\qquad
\begin{array}{r} 2 \\ \times\ 4 \\ \hline \end{array}
\qquad
\begin{array}{r} 2 \\ \times\ 2 \\ \hline \end{array}
\qquad
\begin{array}{r} 2 \\ \times\ 5 \\ \hline \end{array}
$$

$$
\begin{array}{r} 2 \\ \times\ 5 \\ \hline \end{array}
\qquad
\begin{array}{r} 3 \\ \times\ 2 \\ \hline \end{array}
\qquad
\begin{array}{r} 5 \\ \times\ 2 \\ \hline \end{array}
\qquad
\begin{array}{r} 1 \\ \times\ 1 \\ \hline \end{array}
\qquad
\begin{array}{r} 4 \\ \times\ 2 \\ \hline \end{array}
$$

$$
\begin{array}{r} 2 \\ \times\ 4 \\ \hline \end{array}
\qquad
\begin{array}{r} 5 \\ \times\ 2 \\ \hline \end{array}
\qquad
\begin{array}{r} 2 \\ \times\ 2 \\ \hline \end{array}
\qquad
\begin{array}{r} 2 \\ \times\ 5 \\ \hline \end{array}
\qquad
\begin{array}{r} 3 \\ \times\ 2 \\ \hline \end{array}
$$

2	2	6	3	2
x 5	x 4	x 2	x 0	x 6

2	2	2	6	5
x 2	x 6	x 3	x 2	x 2

6	2	2	1	4
x 2	x 5	x 6	x 2	x 2

4	2	5	2	6
x 1	x 6	x 2	x 2	x 2

6	3	2	1	2
x 2	x 2	x 6	x 7	x 5

5	2	2	6	2
x 2	x 6	x 4	x 2	x 3

$$\begin{array}{r} 6 \\ \times\ 2 \\ \hline \end{array} \qquad \begin{array}{r} 3 \\ \times\ 2 \\ \hline \end{array} \qquad \begin{array}{r} 2 \\ \times\ 7 \\ \hline \end{array} \qquad \begin{array}{r} 5 \\ \times\ 2 \\ \hline \end{array} \qquad \begin{array}{r} 7 \\ \times\ 2 \\ \hline \end{array}$$

$$\begin{array}{r} 2 \\ \times\ 4 \\ \hline \end{array} \qquad \begin{array}{r} 7 \\ \times\ 2 \\ \hline \end{array} \qquad \begin{array}{r} 2 \\ \times\ 2 \\ \hline \end{array} \qquad \begin{array}{r} 2 \\ \times\ 7 \\ \hline \end{array} \qquad \begin{array}{r} 2 \\ \times\ 6 \\ \hline \end{array}$$

$$\begin{array}{r} 2 \\ \times\ 7 \\ \hline \end{array} \qquad \begin{array}{r} 6 \\ \times\ 2 \\ \hline \end{array} \qquad \begin{array}{r} 7 \\ \times\ 2 \\ \hline \end{array} \qquad \begin{array}{r} 0 \\ \times\ 9 \\ \hline \end{array} \qquad \begin{array}{r} 2 \\ \times\ 5 \\ \hline \end{array}$$

$$\begin{array}{r} 2 \\ \times\ 3 \\ \hline \end{array} \qquad \begin{array}{r} 7 \\ \times\ 2 \\ \hline \end{array} \qquad \begin{array}{r} 2 \\ \times\ 6 \\ \hline \end{array} \qquad \begin{array}{r} 4 \\ \times\ 2 \\ \hline \end{array} \qquad \begin{array}{r} 2 \\ \times\ 7 \\ \hline \end{array}$$

$$\begin{array}{r} 2 \\ \times\ 7 \\ \hline \end{array} \qquad \begin{array}{r} 5 \\ \times\ 2 \\ \hline \end{array} \qquad \begin{array}{r} 7 \\ \times\ 2 \\ \hline \end{array} \qquad \begin{array}{r} 2 \\ \times\ 2 \\ \hline \end{array} \qquad \begin{array}{r} 6 \\ \times\ 2 \\ \hline \end{array}$$

$$\begin{array}{r} 2 \\ \times\ 6 \\ \hline \end{array} \qquad \begin{array}{r} 7 \\ \times\ 2 \\ \hline \end{array} \qquad \begin{array}{r} 2 \\ \times\ 4 \\ \hline \end{array} \qquad \begin{array}{r} 2 \\ \times\ 7 \\ \hline \end{array} \qquad \begin{array}{r} 8 \\ \times\ 1 \\ \hline \end{array}$$

Name _____

2 x 7	5 x 2	2 x 8	6 x 2	8 x 2
2 x 6	8 x 2	2 x 2	2 x 8	7 x 2
2 x 8	2 x 7	8 x 2	4 x 2	2 x 6
3 x 2	2 x 8	7 x 2	2 x 5	8 x 2
8 x 2	2 x 4	2 x 8	6 x 2	2 x 7
7 x 2	2 x 8	5 x 2	8 x 2	4 x 2

Name _____

2 x 8	2 x 7	9 x 2	2 x 6	2 x 9
5 x 2	2 x 9	2 x 3	9 x 2	8 x 2
9 x 2	2 x 8	2 x 9	4 x 2	7 x 2
6 x 2	2 x 9	8 x 2	2 x 5	9 x 2
9 x 2	2 x 7	2 x 9	2 x 2	2 x 8
8 x 2	2 x 9	2 x 6	9 x 2	7 x 2

9	2	10	3	2
x 2	x 6	x 2	x 2	x 10

8	2	7	10	2
x 2	x 10	x 2	x 2	x 9

10	9	2	6	2
x 2	x 2	x 10	x 2	x 8

4	2	2	5	10
x 2	x 10	x 9	x 2	x 2

10	8	2	7	9
x 2	x 2	x 10	x 2	x 2

2	2	2	10	2
x 9	x 10	x 7	x 2	x 8

Level A Test
(2 as Factor)

2 × 0	5 × 2	2 × 7	2 × 2	2 × 9
6 × 2	8 × 2	3 × 2	2 × 6	2 × 5
9 × 2	2 × 2	2 × 4	10 × 2	2 × 3
7 × 2	2 × 1	2 × 2	0 × 2	2 × 8
2 × 4	6 × 2	9 × 2	2 × 5	1 × 2
10 × 2	2 × 7	3 × 2	8 × 2	4 × 2

$$
\begin{array}{r} 10 \\ \times\ 2 \\ \hline \end{array}
\qquad
\begin{array}{r} 2 \\ \times\ 8 \\ \hline \end{array}
\qquad
\begin{array}{r} 3 \\ \times\ 2 \\ \hline \end{array}
\qquad
\begin{array}{r} 9 \\ \times\ 2 \\ \hline \end{array}
\qquad
\begin{array}{r} 2 \\ \times\ 3 \\ \hline \end{array}
$$

$$
\begin{array}{r} 6 \\ \times\ 2 \\ \hline \end{array}
\qquad
\begin{array}{r} 2 \\ \times\ 3 \\ \hline \end{array}
\qquad
\begin{array}{r} 7 \\ \times\ 2 \\ \hline \end{array}
\qquad
\begin{array}{r} 3 \\ \times\ 2 \\ \hline \end{array}
\qquad
\begin{array}{r} 2 \\ \times\ 10 \\ \hline \end{array}
$$

$$
\begin{array}{r} 3 \\ \times\ 2 \\ \hline \end{array}
\qquad
\begin{array}{r} 10 \\ \times\ 2 \\ \hline \end{array}
\qquad
\begin{array}{r} 2 \\ \times\ 3 \\ \hline \end{array}
\qquad
\begin{array}{r} 8 \\ \times\ 2 \\ \hline \end{array}
\qquad
\begin{array}{r} 2 \\ \times\ 9 \\ \hline \end{array}
$$

$$
\begin{array}{r} 7 \\ \times\ 2 \\ \hline \end{array}
\qquad
\begin{array}{r} 2 \\ \times\ 3 \\ \hline \end{array}
\qquad
\begin{array}{r} 2 \\ \times\ 10 \\ \hline \end{array}
\qquad
\begin{array}{r} 5 \\ \times\ 2 \\ \hline \end{array}
\qquad
\begin{array}{r} 3 \\ \times\ 2 \\ \hline \end{array}
$$

$$
\begin{array}{r} 3 \\ \times\ 2 \\ \hline \end{array}
\qquad
\begin{array}{r} 9 \\ \times\ 2 \\ \hline \end{array}
\qquad
\begin{array}{r} 2 \\ \times\ 3 \\ \hline \end{array}
\qquad
\begin{array}{r} 2 \\ \times\ 7 \\ \hline \end{array}
\qquad
\begin{array}{r} 10 \\ \times\ 2 \\ \hline \end{array}
$$

$$
\begin{array}{r} 2 \\ \times\ 10 \\ \hline \end{array}
\qquad
\begin{array}{r} 2 \\ \times\ 3 \\ \hline \end{array}
\qquad
\begin{array}{r} 8 \\ \times\ 2 \\ \hline \end{array}
\qquad
\begin{array}{r} 3 \\ \times\ 2 \\ \hline \end{array}
\qquad
\begin{array}{r} 2 \\ \times\ 9 \\ \hline \end{array}
$$

$$\begin{array}{r} 3 \\ \times\ 2 \\ \hline \end{array} \qquad \begin{array}{r} 2 \\ \times\ 8 \\ \hline \end{array} \qquad \begin{array}{r} 3 \\ \times\ 3 \\ \hline \end{array} \qquad \begin{array}{r} 7 \\ \times\ 2 \\ \hline \end{array} \qquad \begin{array}{r} 3 \\ \times\ 3 \\ \hline \end{array}$$

$$\begin{array}{r} 2 \\ \times\ 5 \\ \hline \end{array} \qquad \begin{array}{r} 3 \\ \times\ 3 \\ \hline \end{array} \qquad \begin{array}{r} 9 \\ \times\ 2 \\ \hline \end{array} \qquad \begin{array}{r} 3 \\ \times\ 3 \\ \hline \end{array} \qquad \begin{array}{r} 2 \\ \times\ 3 \\ \hline \end{array}$$

$$\begin{array}{r} 3 \\ \times\ 3 \\ \hline \end{array} \qquad \begin{array}{r} 2 \\ \times\ 7 \\ \hline \end{array} \qquad \begin{array}{r} 3 \\ \times\ 3 \\ \hline \end{array} \qquad \begin{array}{r} 10 \\ \times\ 2 \\ \hline \end{array} \qquad \begin{array}{r} 8 \\ \times\ 2 \\ \hline \end{array}$$

$$\begin{array}{r} 2 \\ \times\ 4 \\ \hline \end{array} \qquad \begin{array}{r} 3 \\ \times\ 3 \\ \hline \end{array} \qquad \begin{array}{r} 3 \\ \times\ 2 \\ \hline \end{array} \qquad \begin{array}{r} 2 \\ \times\ 9 \\ \hline \end{array} \qquad \begin{array}{r} 3 \\ \times\ 3 \\ \hline \end{array}$$

$$\begin{array}{r} 3 \\ \times\ 3 \\ \hline \end{array} \qquad \begin{array}{r} 2 \\ \times\ 6 \\ \hline \end{array} \qquad \begin{array}{r} 3 \\ \times\ 3 \\ \hline \end{array} \qquad \begin{array}{r} 7 \\ \times\ 2 \\ \hline \end{array} \qquad \begin{array}{r} 2 \\ \times\ 3 \\ \hline \end{array}$$

$$\begin{array}{r} 2 \\ \times\ 10 \\ \hline \end{array} \qquad \begin{array}{r} 3 \\ \times\ 3 \\ \hline \end{array} \qquad \begin{array}{r} 2 \\ \times\ 8 \\ \hline \end{array} \qquad \begin{array}{r} 3 \\ \times\ 3 \\ \hline \end{array} \qquad \begin{array}{r} 9 \\ \times\ 2 \\ \hline \end{array}$$

3 x 3	9 x 2	4 x 3	2 x 7	3 x 4
5 x 2	3 x 4	2 x 8	4 x 3	3 x 3
4 x 3	3 x 3	3 x 4	10 x 2	2 x 9
7 x 2	3 x 4	3 x 3	2 x 6	4 x 3
4 x 3	8 x 2	3 x 4	2 x 4	3 x 3
3 x 3	3 x 4	9 x 2	4 x 3	10 x 2

3 x 4	3 x 3	3 x 5	2 x 9	5 x 3
8 x 2	5 x 3	2 x 7	3 x 5	4 x 3
3 x 5	3 x 5	5 x 3	10 x 2	3 x 3
9 x 2	5 x 3	4 x 3	2 x 3	3 x 5
3 x 5	6 x 2	5 x 3	2 x 8	3 x 4
4 x 3	5 x 3	3 x 3	3 x 5	7 x 2

$$
\begin{array}{r} 3 \\ \times\ 5 \\ \hline \end{array}
\qquad
\begin{array}{r} 3 \\ \times\ 3 \\ \hline \end{array}
\qquad
\begin{array}{r} 6 \\ \times\ 3 \\ \hline \end{array}
\qquad
\begin{array}{r} 4 \\ \times\ 3 \\ \hline \end{array}
\qquad
\begin{array}{r} 3 \\ \times\ 6 \\ \hline \end{array}
$$

$$
\begin{array}{r} 2 \\ \times\ 9 \\ \hline \end{array}
\qquad
\begin{array}{r} 3 \\ \times\ 6 \\ \hline \end{array}
\qquad
\begin{array}{r} 8 \\ \times\ 2 \\ \hline \end{array}
\qquad
\begin{array}{r} 6 \\ \times\ 3 \\ \hline \end{array}
\qquad
\begin{array}{r} 3 \\ \times\ 5 \\ \hline \end{array}
$$

$$
\begin{array}{r} 6 \\ \times\ 3 \\ \hline \end{array}
\qquad
\begin{array}{r} 5 \\ \times\ 3 \\ \hline \end{array}
\qquad
\begin{array}{r} 3 \\ \times\ 6 \\ \hline \end{array}
\qquad
\begin{array}{r} 2 \\ \times\ 5 \\ \hline \end{array}
\qquad
\begin{array}{r} 3 \\ \times\ 4 \\ \hline \end{array}
$$

$$
\begin{array}{r} 3 \\ \times\ 3 \\ \hline \end{array}
\qquad
\begin{array}{r} 3 \\ \times\ 6 \\ \hline \end{array}
\qquad
\begin{array}{r} 3 \\ \times\ 5 \\ \hline \end{array}
\qquad
\begin{array}{r} 10 \\ \times\ 2 \\ \hline \end{array}
\qquad
\begin{array}{r} 6 \\ \times\ 3 \\ \hline \end{array}
$$

$$
\begin{array}{r} 6 \\ \times\ 3 \\ \hline \end{array}
\qquad
\begin{array}{r} 4 \\ \times\ 3 \\ \hline \end{array}
\qquad
\begin{array}{r} 3 \\ \times\ 6 \\ \hline \end{array}
\qquad
\begin{array}{r} 2 \\ \times\ 4 \\ \hline \end{array}
\qquad
\begin{array}{r} 5 \\ \times\ 3 \\ \hline \end{array}
$$

$$
\begin{array}{r} 3 \\ \times\ 5 \\ \hline \end{array}
\qquad
\begin{array}{r} 3 \\ \times\ 6 \\ \hline \end{array}
\qquad
\begin{array}{r} 3 \\ \times\ 3 \\ \hline \end{array}
\qquad
\begin{array}{r} 6 \\ \times\ 3 \\ \hline \end{array}
\qquad
\begin{array}{r} 3 \\ \times\ 4 \\ \hline \end{array}
$$

Name _____

$$\begin{array}{r} 6 \\ \times\ 3 \\ \hline \end{array}$$
$$\begin{array}{r} 3 \\ \times\ 3 \\ \hline \end{array}$$
$$\begin{array}{r} 3 \\ \times\ 7 \\ \hline \end{array}$$
$$\begin{array}{r} 3 \\ \times\ 4 \\ \hline \end{array}$$
$$\begin{array}{r} 7 \\ \times\ 3 \\ \hline \end{array}$$

$$\begin{array}{r} 2 \\ \times\ 9 \\ \hline \end{array}$$
$$\begin{array}{r} 7 \\ \times\ 3 \\ \hline \end{array}$$
$$\begin{array}{r} 10 \\ \times\ 2 \\ \hline \end{array}$$
$$\begin{array}{r} 3 \\ \times\ 7 \\ \hline \end{array}$$
$$\begin{array}{r} 3 \\ \times\ 6 \\ \hline \end{array}$$

$$\begin{array}{r} 3 \\ \times\ 7 \\ \hline \end{array}$$
$$\begin{array}{r} 6 \\ \times\ 3 \\ \hline \end{array}$$
$$\begin{array}{r} 7 \\ \times\ 3 \\ \hline \end{array}$$
$$\begin{array}{r} 2 \\ \times\ 7 \\ \hline \end{array}$$
$$\begin{array}{r} 4 \\ \times\ 3 \\ \hline \end{array}$$

$$\begin{array}{r} 3 \\ \times\ 3 \\ \hline \end{array}$$
$$\begin{array}{r} 7 \\ \times\ 3 \\ \hline \end{array}$$
$$\begin{array}{r} 3 \\ \times\ 6 \\ \hline \end{array}$$
$$\begin{array}{r} 2 \\ \times\ 8 \\ \hline \end{array}$$
$$\begin{array}{r} 3 \\ \times\ 7 \\ \hline \end{array}$$

$$\begin{array}{r} 3 \\ \times\ 7 \\ \hline \end{array}$$
$$\begin{array}{r} 3 \\ \times\ 4 \\ \hline \end{array}$$
$$\begin{array}{r} 7 \\ \times\ 3 \\ \hline \end{array}$$
$$\begin{array}{r} 2 \\ \times\ 6 \\ \hline \end{array}$$
$$\begin{array}{r} 6 \\ \times\ 3 \\ \hline \end{array}$$

$$\begin{array}{r} 3 \\ \times\ 6 \\ \hline \end{array}$$
$$\begin{array}{r} 7 \\ \times\ 3 \\ \hline \end{array}$$
$$\begin{array}{r} 9 \\ \times\ 2 \\ \hline \end{array}$$
$$\begin{array}{r} 3 \\ \times\ 7 \\ \hline \end{array}$$
$$\begin{array}{r} 3 \\ \times\ 3 \\ \hline \end{array}$$

Name _____

$$\begin{array}{r} 7 \\ \times\ 3 \\ \hline \end{array} \qquad \begin{array}{r} 5 \\ \times\ 2 \\ \hline \end{array} \qquad \begin{array}{r} 8 \\ \times\ 3 \\ \hline \end{array} \qquad \begin{array}{r} 3 \\ \times\ 5 \\ \hline \end{array} \qquad \begin{array}{r} 3 \\ \times\ 8 \\ \hline \end{array}$$

$$\begin{array}{r} 2 \\ \times\ 2 \\ \hline \end{array} \qquad \begin{array}{r} 3 \\ \times\ 8 \\ \hline \end{array} \qquad \begin{array}{r} 3 \\ \times\ 6 \\ \hline \end{array} \qquad \begin{array}{r} 8 \\ \times\ 3 \\ \hline \end{array} \qquad \begin{array}{r} 3 \\ \times\ 7 \\ \hline \end{array}$$

$$\begin{array}{r} 8 \\ \times\ 3 \\ \hline \end{array} \qquad \begin{array}{r} 3 \\ \times\ 7 \\ \hline \end{array} \qquad \begin{array}{r} 3 \\ \times\ 8 \\ \hline \end{array} \qquad \begin{array}{r} 4 \\ \times\ 3 \\ \hline \end{array} \qquad \begin{array}{r} 6 \\ \times\ 3 \\ \hline \end{array}$$

$$\begin{array}{r} 5 \\ \times\ 3 \\ \hline \end{array} \qquad \begin{array}{r} 3 \\ \times\ 8 \\ \hline \end{array} \qquad \begin{array}{r} 7 \\ \times\ 3 \\ \hline \end{array} \qquad \begin{array}{r} 3 \\ \times\ 2 \\ \hline \end{array} \qquad \begin{array}{r} 8 \\ \times\ 3 \\ \hline \end{array}$$

$$\begin{array}{r} 8 \\ \times\ 3 \\ \hline \end{array} \qquad \begin{array}{r} 3 \\ \times\ 6 \\ \hline \end{array} \qquad \begin{array}{r} 3 \\ \times\ 8 \\ \hline \end{array} \qquad \begin{array}{r} 4 \\ \times\ 2 \\ \hline \end{array} \qquad \begin{array}{r} 3 \\ \times\ 7 \\ \hline \end{array}$$

$$\begin{array}{r} 7 \\ \times\ 3 \\ \hline \end{array} \qquad \begin{array}{r} 3 \\ \times\ 8 \\ \hline \end{array} \qquad \begin{array}{r} 3 \\ \times\ 3 \\ \hline \end{array} \qquad \begin{array}{r} 8 \\ \times\ 3 \\ \hline \end{array} \qquad \begin{array}{r} 3 \\ \times\ 5 \\ \hline \end{array}$$

$$
\begin{array}{r} 8 \\ \times\ 3 \\ \hline \end{array}
\qquad
\begin{array}{r} 3 \\ \times\ 7 \\ \hline \end{array}
\qquad
\begin{array}{r} 9 \\ \times\ 3 \\ \hline \end{array}
\qquad
\begin{array}{r} 3 \\ \times\ 4 \\ \hline \end{array}
\qquad
\begin{array}{r} 3 \\ \times\ 9 \\ \hline \end{array}
$$

$$
\begin{array}{r} 3 \\ \times\ 6 \\ \hline \end{array}
\qquad
\begin{array}{r} 3 \\ \times\ 9 \\ \hline \end{array}
\qquad
\begin{array}{r} 8 \\ \times\ 2 \\ \hline \end{array}
\qquad
\begin{array}{r} 9 \\ \times\ 3 \\ \hline \end{array}
\qquad
\begin{array}{r} 3 \\ \times\ 8 \\ \hline \end{array}
$$

$$
\begin{array}{r} 9 \\ \times\ 3 \\ \hline \end{array}
\qquad
\begin{array}{r} 8 \\ \times\ 3 \\ \hline \end{array}
\qquad
\begin{array}{r} 3 \\ \times\ 9 \\ \hline \end{array}
\qquad
\begin{array}{r} 6 \\ \times\ 3 \\ \hline \end{array}
\qquad
\begin{array}{r} 3 \\ \times\ 7 \\ \hline \end{array}
$$

$$
\begin{array}{r} 3 \\ \times\ 3 \\ \hline \end{array}
\qquad
\begin{array}{r} 3 \\ \times\ 9 \\ \hline \end{array}
\qquad
\begin{array}{r} 3 \\ \times\ 8 \\ \hline \end{array}
\qquad
\begin{array}{r} 2 \\ \times\ 9 \\ \hline \end{array}
\qquad
\begin{array}{r} 9 \\ \times\ 3 \\ \hline \end{array}
$$

$$
\begin{array}{r} 9 \\ \times\ 3 \\ \hline \end{array}
\qquad
\begin{array}{r} 7 \\ \times\ 3 \\ \hline \end{array}
\qquad
\begin{array}{r} 3 \\ \times\ 9 \\ \hline \end{array}
\qquad
\begin{array}{r} 5 \\ \times\ 3 \\ \hline \end{array}
\qquad
\begin{array}{r} 8 \\ \times\ 3 \\ \hline \end{array}
$$

$$
\begin{array}{r} 3 \\ \times\ 8 \\ \hline \end{array}
\qquad
\begin{array}{r} 3 \\ \times\ 9 \\ \hline \end{array}
\qquad
\begin{array}{r} 3 \\ \times\ 6 \\ \hline \end{array}
\qquad
\begin{array}{r} 9 \\ \times\ 3 \\ \hline \end{array}
\qquad
\begin{array}{r} 7 \\ \times\ 3 \\ \hline \end{array}
$$

Name _____

3 x 9	3 x 7	10 x 3	3 x 8	10 x 3
6 x 3	10 x 3	3 x 5	10 x 3	9 x 3
10 x 3	3 x 9	10 x 3	7 x 2	8 x 3
3 x 3	10 x 3	9 x 3	3 x 7	10 x 3
10 x 3	3 x 8	10 x 3	4 x 3	3 x 9
9 x 3	10 x 3	8 x 3	10 x 3	3 x 6

3 × 8	6 × 3	10 × 3	3 × 3	3 × 9
3 × 1	4 × 3	3 × 7	2 × 3	3 × 5
3 × 3	9 × 3	1 × 3	3 × 6	0 × 3
10 × 3	7 × 3	3 × 0	8 × 3	3 × 4
5 × 3	3 × 2	6 × 3	3 × 9	3 × 3
4 × 3	3 × 8	3 × 5	3 × 7	10 × 3

$$
\begin{array}{r} 10 \\ \times\ 3 \\ \hline \end{array}
\qquad
\begin{array}{r} 8 \\ \times\ 3 \\ \hline \end{array}
\qquad
\begin{array}{r} 2 \\ \times\ 4 \\ \hline \end{array}
\qquad
\begin{array}{r} 9 \\ \times\ 3 \\ \hline \end{array}
\qquad
\begin{array}{r} 4 \\ \times\ 2 \\ \hline \end{array}
$$

$$
\begin{array}{r} 3 \\ \times\ 7 \\ \hline \end{array}
\qquad
\begin{array}{r} 4 \\ \times\ 2 \\ \hline \end{array}
\qquad
\begin{array}{r} 6 \\ \times\ 3 \\ \hline \end{array}
\qquad
\begin{array}{r} 2 \\ \times\ 4 \\ \hline \end{array}
\qquad
\begin{array}{r} 10 \\ \times\ 3 \\ \hline \end{array}
$$

$$
\begin{array}{r} 2 \\ \times\ 4 \\ \hline \end{array}
\qquad
\begin{array}{r} 10 \\ \times\ 3 \\ \hline \end{array}
\qquad
\begin{array}{r} 4 \\ \times\ 2 \\ \hline \end{array}
\qquad
\begin{array}{r} 2 \\ \times\ 6 \\ \hline \end{array}
\qquad
\begin{array}{r} 3 \\ \times\ 9 \\ \hline \end{array}
$$

$$
\begin{array}{r} 5 \\ \times\ 3 \\ \hline \end{array}
\qquad
\begin{array}{r} 4 \\ \times\ 2 \\ \hline \end{array}
\qquad
\begin{array}{r} 10 \\ \times\ 3 \\ \hline \end{array}
\qquad
\begin{array}{r} 3 \\ \times\ 8 \\ \hline \end{array}
\qquad
\begin{array}{r} 2 \\ \times\ 4 \\ \hline \end{array}
$$

$$
\begin{array}{r} 4 \\ \times\ 2 \\ \hline \end{array}
\qquad
\begin{array}{r} 9 \\ \times\ 3 \\ \hline \end{array}
\qquad
\begin{array}{r} 2 \\ \times\ 4 \\ \hline \end{array}
\qquad
\begin{array}{r} 3 \\ \times\ 6 \\ \hline \end{array}
\qquad
\begin{array}{r} 10 \\ \times\ 3 \\ \hline \end{array}
$$

$$
\begin{array}{r} 10 \\ \times\ 3 \\ \hline \end{array}
\qquad
\begin{array}{r} 4 \\ \times\ 2 \\ \hline \end{array}
\qquad
\begin{array}{r} 8 \\ \times\ 3 \\ \hline \end{array}
\qquad
\begin{array}{r} 2 \\ \times\ 4 \\ \hline \end{array}
\qquad
\begin{array}{r} 7 \\ \times\ 3 \\ \hline \end{array}
$$

Name _____

$$\begin{array}{r} 4 \\ \times\ 2 \\ \hline \end{array} \qquad \begin{array}{r} 8 \\ \times\ 3 \\ \hline \end{array} \qquad \begin{array}{r} 3 \\ \times\ 4 \\ \hline \end{array} \qquad \begin{array}{r} 3 \\ \times\ 3 \\ \hline \end{array} \qquad \begin{array}{r} 4 \\ \times\ 3 \\ \hline \end{array}$$

$$\begin{array}{r} 3 \\ \times\ 7 \\ \hline \end{array} \qquad \begin{array}{r} 4 \\ \times\ 3 \\ \hline \end{array} \qquad \begin{array}{r} 6 \\ \times\ 3 \\ \hline \end{array} \qquad \begin{array}{r} 3 \\ \times\ 4 \\ \hline \end{array} \qquad \begin{array}{r} 2 \\ \times\ 4 \\ \hline \end{array}$$

$$\begin{array}{r} 3 \\ \times\ 4 \\ \hline \end{array} \qquad \begin{array}{r} 3 \\ \times\ 3 \\ \hline \end{array} \qquad \begin{array}{r} 4 \\ \times\ 3 \\ \hline \end{array} \qquad \begin{array}{r} 3 \\ \times\ 8 \\ \hline \end{array} \qquad \begin{array}{r} 10 \\ \times\ 3 \\ \hline \end{array}$$

$$\begin{array}{r} 2 \\ \times\ 8 \\ \hline \end{array} \qquad \begin{array}{r} 4 \\ \times\ 3 \\ \hline \end{array} \qquad \begin{array}{r} 4 \\ \times\ 2 \\ \hline \end{array} \qquad \begin{array}{r} 9 \\ \times\ 3 \\ \hline \end{array} \qquad \begin{array}{r} 3 \\ \times\ 4 \\ \hline \end{array}$$

$$\begin{array}{r} 3 \\ \times\ 4 \\ \hline \end{array} \qquad \begin{array}{r} 3 \\ \times\ 6 \\ \hline \end{array} \qquad \begin{array}{r} 4 \\ \times\ 3 \\ \hline \end{array} \qquad \begin{array}{r} 3 \\ \times\ 5 \\ \hline \end{array} \qquad \begin{array}{r} 7 \\ \times\ 3 \\ \hline \end{array}$$

$$\begin{array}{r} 2 \\ \times\ 4 \\ \hline \end{array} \qquad \begin{array}{r} 4 \\ \times\ 3 \\ \hline \end{array} \qquad \begin{array}{r} 3 \\ \times\ 9 \\ \hline \end{array} \qquad \begin{array}{r} 3 \\ \times\ 4 \\ \hline \end{array} \qquad \begin{array}{r} 10 \\ \times\ 3 \\ \hline \end{array}$$

$$\begin{array}{r} 4 \\ \times\ 3 \\ \hline \end{array} \qquad \begin{array}{r} 3 \\ \times\ 9 \\ \hline \end{array} \qquad \begin{array}{r} 4 \\ \times\ 4 \\ \hline \end{array} \qquad \begin{array}{r} 8 \\ \times\ 3 \\ \hline \end{array} \qquad \begin{array}{r} 4 \\ \times\ 4 \\ \hline \end{array}$$

$$\begin{array}{r} 3 \\ \times\ 7 \\ \hline \end{array} \qquad \begin{array}{r} 4 \\ \times\ 4 \\ \hline \end{array} \qquad \begin{array}{r} 6 \\ \times\ 3 \\ \hline \end{array} \qquad \begin{array}{r} 4 \\ \times\ 4 \\ \hline \end{array} \qquad \begin{array}{r} 3 \\ \times\ 4 \\ \hline \end{array}$$

$$\begin{array}{r} 4 \\ \times\ 4 \\ \hline \end{array} \qquad \begin{array}{r} 3 \\ \times\ 4 \\ \hline \end{array} \qquad \begin{array}{r} 4 \\ \times\ 4 \\ \hline \end{array} \qquad \begin{array}{r} 2 \\ \times\ 4 \\ \hline \end{array} \qquad \begin{array}{r} 9 \\ \times\ 3 \\ \hline \end{array}$$

$$\begin{array}{r} 3 \\ \times\ 8 \\ \hline \end{array} \qquad \begin{array}{r} 4 \\ \times\ 4 \\ \hline \end{array} \qquad \begin{array}{r} 10 \\ \times\ 3 \\ \hline \end{array} \qquad \begin{array}{r} 3 \\ \times\ 5 \\ \hline \end{array} \qquad \begin{array}{r} 4 \\ \times\ 4 \\ \hline \end{array}$$

$$\begin{array}{r} 4 \\ \times\ 4 \\ \hline \end{array} \qquad \begin{array}{r} 7 \\ \times\ 3 \\ \hline \end{array} \qquad \begin{array}{r} 4 \\ \times\ 4 \\ \hline \end{array} \qquad \begin{array}{r} 3 \\ \times\ 6 \\ \hline \end{array} \qquad \begin{array}{r} 4 \\ \times\ 3 \\ \hline \end{array}$$

$$\begin{array}{r} 3 \\ \times\ 4 \\ \hline \end{array} \qquad \begin{array}{r} 4 \\ \times\ 4 \\ \hline \end{array} \qquad \begin{array}{r} 3 \\ \times\ 9 \\ \hline \end{array} \qquad \begin{array}{r} 4 \\ \times\ 4 \\ \hline \end{array} \qquad \begin{array}{r} 8 \\ \times\ 3 \\ \hline \end{array}$$

$$\begin{array}{r} 4 \\ \times\ 4 \\ \hline \end{array} \qquad \begin{array}{r} 3 \\ \times\ 6 \\ \hline \end{array} \qquad \begin{array}{r} 5 \\ \times\ 4 \\ \hline \end{array} \qquad \begin{array}{r} 7 \\ \times\ 3 \\ \hline \end{array} \qquad \begin{array}{r} 4 \\ \times\ 5 \\ \hline \end{array}$$

$$\begin{array}{r} 9 \\ \times\ 3 \\ \hline \end{array} \qquad \begin{array}{r} 4 \\ \times\ 5 \\ \hline \end{array} \qquad \begin{array}{r} 7 \\ \times\ 2 \\ \hline \end{array} \qquad \begin{array}{r} 5 \\ \times\ 4 \\ \hline \end{array} \qquad \begin{array}{r} 4 \\ \times\ 4 \\ \hline \end{array}$$

$$\begin{array}{r} 5 \\ \times\ 4 \\ \hline \end{array} \qquad \begin{array}{r} 4 \\ \times\ 4 \\ \hline \end{array} \qquad \begin{array}{r} 4 \\ \times\ 5 \\ \hline \end{array} \qquad \begin{array}{r} 3 \\ \times\ 8 \\ \hline \end{array} \qquad \begin{array}{r} 4 \\ \times\ 3 \\ \hline \end{array}$$

$$\begin{array}{r} 3 \\ \times\ 7 \\ \hline \end{array} \qquad \begin{array}{r} 4 \\ \times\ 5 \\ \hline \end{array} \qquad \begin{array}{r} 4 \\ \times\ 4 \\ \hline \end{array} \qquad \begin{array}{r} 10 \\ \times\ 3 \\ \hline \end{array} \qquad \begin{array}{r} 5 \\ \times\ 4 \\ \hline \end{array}$$

$$\begin{array}{r} 5 \\ \times\ 4 \\ \hline \end{array} \qquad \begin{array}{r} 3 \\ \times\ 9 \\ \hline \end{array} \qquad \begin{array}{r} 4 \\ \times\ 5 \\ \hline \end{array} \qquad \begin{array}{r} 6 \\ \times\ 3 \\ \hline \end{array} \qquad \begin{array}{r} 4 \\ \times\ 4 \\ \hline \end{array}$$

$$\begin{array}{r} 4 \\ \times\ 4 \\ \hline \end{array} \qquad \begin{array}{r} 4 \\ \times\ 5 \\ \hline \end{array} \qquad \begin{array}{r} 8 \\ \times\ 3 \\ \hline \end{array} \qquad \begin{array}{r} 5 \\ \times\ 4 \\ \hline \end{array} \qquad \begin{array}{r} 4 \\ \times\ 2 \\ \hline \end{array}$$

Name _____

```
    5        4        6        3        4
  x 4      x 4      x 4      x 7      x 6
```

```
    9        4       10        6        4
  x 3      x 6      x 2      x 4      x 5
```

```
    6        4        4        2        4
  x 4      x 5      x 6      x 4      x 4
```

```
    8        4        5       10        6
  x 3      x 6      x 4      x 3      x 4
```

```
    6        4        4        3        4
  x 4      x 4      x 6      x 4      x 5
```

```
    5        4        4        6        3
  x 4      x 6      x 4      x 4      x 9
```

Name _____

$$\begin{array}{r} 6 \\ \times\ 4 \\ \hline \end{array}$$
$$\begin{array}{r} 4 \\ \times\ 4 \\ \hline \end{array}$$
$$\begin{array}{r} 4 \\ \times\ 7 \\ \hline \end{array}$$
$$\begin{array}{r} 5 \\ \times\ 4 \\ \hline \end{array}$$
$$\begin{array}{r} 7 \\ \times\ 4 \\ \hline \end{array}$$

$$\begin{array}{r} 6 \\ \times\ 3 \\ \hline \end{array}$$
$$\begin{array}{r} 7 \\ \times\ 4 \\ \hline \end{array}$$
$$\begin{array}{r} 8 \\ \times\ 3 \\ \hline \end{array}$$
$$\begin{array}{r} 4 \\ \times\ 7 \\ \hline \end{array}$$
$$\begin{array}{r} 4 \\ \times\ 6 \\ \hline \end{array}$$

$$\begin{array}{r} 4 \\ \times\ 7 \\ \hline \end{array}$$
$$\begin{array}{r} 6 \\ \times\ 4 \\ \hline \end{array}$$
$$\begin{array}{r} 7 \\ \times\ 4 \\ \hline \end{array}$$
$$\begin{array}{r} 4 \\ \times\ 4 \\ \hline \end{array}$$
$$\begin{array}{r} 4 \\ \times\ 5 \\ \hline \end{array}$$

$$\begin{array}{r} 4 \\ \times\ 2 \\ \hline \end{array}$$
$$\begin{array}{r} 7 \\ \times\ 4 \\ \hline \end{array}$$
$$\begin{array}{r} 4 \\ \times\ 6 \\ \hline \end{array}$$
$$\begin{array}{r} 10 \\ \times\ 3 \\ \hline \end{array}$$
$$\begin{array}{r} 4 \\ \times\ 7 \\ \hline \end{array}$$

$$\begin{array}{r} 4 \\ \times\ 7 \\ \hline \end{array}$$
$$\begin{array}{r} 4 \\ \times\ 5 \\ \hline \end{array}$$
$$\begin{array}{r} 7 \\ \times\ 4 \\ \hline \end{array}$$
$$\begin{array}{r} 4 \\ \times\ 3 \\ \hline \end{array}$$
$$\begin{array}{r} 6 \\ \times\ 4 \\ \hline \end{array}$$

$$\begin{array}{r} 4 \\ \times\ 6 \\ \hline \end{array}$$
$$\begin{array}{r} 7 \\ \times\ 4 \\ \hline \end{array}$$
$$\begin{array}{r} 4 \\ \times\ 4 \\ \hline \end{array}$$
$$\begin{array}{r} 4 \\ \times\ 7 \\ \hline \end{array}$$
$$\begin{array}{r} 9 \\ \times\ 3 \\ \hline \end{array}$$

Name _____

7 x 4	3 x 8	8 x 4	6 x 4	4 x 8
3 x 5	4 x 8	4 x 4	8 x 4	4 x 7
8 x 4	4 x 7	4 x 8	5 x 4	4 x 6
4 x 4	4 x 8	7 x 4	3 x 9	8 x 4
8 x 4	6 x 4	4 x 8	3 x 6	4 x 7
7 x 4	4 x 8	4 x 6	8 x 4	4 x 5

Name _____

8 x 4	4 x 5	4 x 9	7 x 4	9 x 4
4 x 4	9 x 4	6 x 4	4 x 9	4 x 8
4 x 9	8 x 4	9 x 4	7 x 3	4 x 7
6 x 4	9 x 4	4 x 8	4 x 4	4 x 9
4 x 9	7 x 4	9 x 4	4 x 6	8 x 4
4 x 8	9 x 4	5 x 4	4 x 9	3 x 6

4 x 9	4 x 4	10 x 4	4 x 8	10 x 4
4 x 7	10 x 4	9 x 4	10 x 4	4 x 6
10 x 4	4 x 5	10 x 4	7 x 4	4 x 9
8 x 4	10 x 4	9 x 4	4 x 3	10 x 4
10 x 4	4 x 7	10 x 4	4 x 9	4 x 8
9 x 4	10 x 4	4 x 8	10 x 4	6 x 4

Level A Test
(4 as Factor)

Name _____

8 × 4	4 × 1	10 × 4	5 × 4	4 × 7
4 × 3	6 × 4	4 × 4	4 × 9	2 × 4
4 × 5	10 × 4	7 × 4	4 × 0	4 × 8
9 × 4	4 × 4	3 × 4	4 × 6	1 × 4
4 × 2	4 × 5	8 × 4	4 × 3	10 × 4
0 × 4	4 × 7	4 × 9	4 × 4	6 × 4

$$
\begin{array}{r} 10 \\ \times\ 4 \\ \hline \end{array}
\qquad
\begin{array}{r} 4 \\ \times\ 7 \\ \hline \end{array}
\qquad
\begin{array}{r} 2 \\ \times\ 5 \\ \hline \end{array}
\qquad
\begin{array}{r} 9 \\ \times\ 4 \\ \hline \end{array}
\qquad
\begin{array}{r} 5 \\ \times\ 2 \\ \hline \end{array}
$$

$$
\begin{array}{r} 4 \\ \times\ 5 \\ \hline \end{array}
\qquad
\begin{array}{r} 5 \\ \times\ 2 \\ \hline \end{array}
\qquad
\begin{array}{r} 10 \\ \times\ 4 \\ \hline \end{array}
\qquad
\begin{array}{r} 2 \\ \times\ 5 \\ \hline \end{array}
\qquad
\begin{array}{r} 6 \\ \times\ 4 \\ \hline \end{array}
$$

$$
\begin{array}{r} 2 \\ \times\ 5 \\ \hline \end{array}
\qquad
\begin{array}{r} 4 \\ \times\ 9 \\ \hline \end{array}
\qquad
\begin{array}{r} 5 \\ \times\ 2 \\ \hline \end{array}
\qquad
\begin{array}{r} 4 \\ \times\ 8 \\ \hline \end{array}
\qquad
\begin{array}{r} 10 \\ \times\ 4 \\ \hline \end{array}
$$

$$
\begin{array}{r} 4 \\ \times\ 6 \\ \hline \end{array}
\qquad
\begin{array}{r} 5 \\ \times\ 2 \\ \hline \end{array}
\qquad
\begin{array}{r} 10 \\ \times\ 4 \\ \hline \end{array}
\qquad
\begin{array}{r} 7 \\ \times\ 4 \\ \hline \end{array}
\qquad
\begin{array}{r} 2 \\ \times\ 5 \\ \hline \end{array}
$$

$$
\begin{array}{r} 2 \\ \times\ 5 \\ \hline \end{array}
\qquad
\begin{array}{r} 8 \\ \times\ 4 \\ \hline \end{array}
\qquad
\begin{array}{r} 5 \\ \times\ 2 \\ \hline \end{array}
\qquad
\begin{array}{r} 10 \\ \times\ 4 \\ \hline \end{array}
\qquad
\begin{array}{r} 9 \\ \times\ 4 \\ \hline \end{array}
$$

$$
\begin{array}{r} 10 \\ \times\ 4 \\ \hline \end{array}
\qquad
\begin{array}{r} 5 \\ \times\ 2 \\ \hline \end{array}
\qquad
\begin{array}{r} 4 \\ \times\ 9 \\ \hline \end{array}
\qquad
\begin{array}{r} 2 \\ \times\ 5 \\ \hline \end{array}
\qquad
\begin{array}{r} 4 \\ \times\ 8 \\ \hline \end{array}
$$

Name _____

$$\begin{array}{r} 2 \\ \times\ 5 \\ \hline \end{array} \qquad \begin{array}{r} 9 \\ \times\ 4 \\ \hline \end{array} \qquad \begin{array}{r} 5 \\ \times\ 3 \\ \hline \end{array} \qquad \begin{array}{r} 4 \\ \times\ 8 \\ \hline \end{array} \qquad \begin{array}{r} 3 \\ \times\ 5 \\ \hline \end{array}$$

$$\begin{array}{r} 4 \\ \times\ 7 \\ \hline \end{array} \qquad \begin{array}{r} 3 \\ \times\ 5 \\ \hline \end{array} \qquad \begin{array}{r} 1 \\ \times\ 5 \\ \hline \end{array} \qquad \begin{array}{r} 5 \\ \times\ 3 \\ \hline \end{array} \qquad \begin{array}{r} 3 \\ \times\ 9 \\ \hline \end{array}$$

$$\begin{array}{r} 5 \\ \times\ 3 \\ \hline \end{array} \qquad \begin{array}{r} 10 \\ \times\ 4 \\ \hline \end{array} \qquad \begin{array}{r} 3 \\ \times\ 5 \\ \hline \end{array} \qquad \begin{array}{r} 4 \\ \times\ 9 \\ \hline \end{array} \qquad \begin{array}{r} 5 \\ \times\ 2 \\ \hline \end{array}$$

$$\begin{array}{r} 8 \\ \times\ 4 \\ \hline \end{array} \qquad \begin{array}{r} 3 \\ \times\ 5 \\ \hline \end{array} \qquad \begin{array}{r} 5 \\ \times\ 0 \\ \hline \end{array} \qquad \begin{array}{r} 7 \\ \times\ 4 \\ \hline \end{array} \qquad \begin{array}{r} 5 \\ \times\ 3 \\ \hline \end{array}$$

$$\begin{array}{r} 5 \\ \times\ 3 \\ \hline \end{array} \qquad \begin{array}{r} 9 \\ \times\ 4 \\ \hline \end{array} \qquad \begin{array}{r} 3 \\ \times\ 5 \\ \hline \end{array} \qquad \begin{array}{r} 2 \\ \times\ 5 \\ \hline \end{array} \qquad \begin{array}{r} 4 \\ \times\ 8 \\ \hline \end{array}$$

$$\begin{array}{r} 5 \\ \times\ 2 \\ \hline \end{array} \qquad \begin{array}{r} 3 \\ \times\ 5 \\ \hline \end{array} \qquad \begin{array}{r} 4 \\ \times\ 6 \\ \hline \end{array} \qquad \begin{array}{r} 5 \\ \times\ 3 \\ \hline \end{array} \qquad \begin{array}{r} 10 \\ \times\ 4 \\ \hline \end{array}$$

Name _____

5 x 3	3 x 7	5 x 4	6 x 4	4 x 5
7 x 4	4 x 5	10 x 4	5 x 4	4 x 8
5 x 4	4 x 4	4 x 5	8 x 3	3 x 5
9 x 4	4 x 5	5 x 3	4 x 7	5 x 4
5 x 4	8 x 4	4 x 5	5 x 2	4 x 4
4 x 6	4 x 5	9 x 4	5 x 4	3 x 5

4 x 5	3 x 9	5 x 5	4 x 8	5 x 5
4 x 7	5 x 5	3 x 5	5 x 5	10 x 4
5 x 5	6 x 3	5 x 5	4 x 4	5 x 4
9 x 4	5 x 5	0 x 5	6 x 4	5 x 5
5 x 5	7 x 4	5 x 5	4 x 5	8 x 4
5 x 4	5 x 5	4 x 9	5 x 5	5 x 2

$$
\begin{array}{r} 5 \\ \times\ 5 \\ \hline \end{array}
\qquad
\begin{array}{r} 4 \\ \times\ 6 \\ \hline \end{array}
\qquad
\begin{array}{r} 6 \\ \times\ 5 \\ \hline \end{array}
\qquad
\begin{array}{r} 9 \\ \times\ 4 \\ \hline \end{array}
\qquad
\begin{array}{r} 5 \\ \times\ 6 \\ \hline \end{array}
$$

$$
\begin{array}{r} 4 \\ \times\ 4 \\ \hline \end{array}
\qquad
\begin{array}{r} 5 \\ \times\ 6 \\ \hline \end{array}
\qquad
\begin{array}{r} 5 \\ \times\ 5 \\ \hline \end{array}
\qquad
\begin{array}{r} 6 \\ \times\ 5 \\ \hline \end{array}
\qquad
\begin{array}{r} 5 \\ \times\ 3 \\ \hline \end{array}
$$

$$
\begin{array}{r} 6 \\ \times\ 5 \\ \hline \end{array}
\qquad
\begin{array}{r} 8 \\ \times\ 4 \\ \hline \end{array}
\qquad
\begin{array}{r} 5 \\ \times\ 6 \\ \hline \end{array}
\qquad
\begin{array}{r} 3 \\ \times\ 3 \\ \hline \end{array}
\qquad
\begin{array}{r} 5 \\ \times\ 5 \\ \hline \end{array}
$$

$$
\begin{array}{r} 10 \\ \times\ 4 \\ \hline \end{array}
\qquad
\begin{array}{r} 5 \\ \times\ 6 \\ \hline \end{array}
\qquad
\begin{array}{r} 5 \\ \times\ 5 \\ \hline \end{array}
\qquad
\begin{array}{r} 7 \\ \times\ 4 \\ \hline \end{array}
\qquad
\begin{array}{r} 6 \\ \times\ 5 \\ \hline \end{array}
$$

$$
\begin{array}{r} 6 \\ \times\ 5 \\ \hline \end{array}
\qquad
\begin{array}{r} 4 \\ \times\ 3 \\ \hline \end{array}
\qquad
\begin{array}{r} 5 \\ \times\ 6 \\ \hline \end{array}
\qquad
\begin{array}{r} 5 \\ \times\ 5 \\ \hline \end{array}
\qquad
\begin{array}{r} 4 \\ \times\ 9 \\ \hline \end{array}
$$

$$
\begin{array}{r} 5 \\ \times\ 5 \\ \hline \end{array}
\qquad
\begin{array}{r} 5 \\ \times\ 6 \\ \hline \end{array}
\qquad
\begin{array}{r} 5 \\ \times\ 4 \\ \hline \end{array}
\qquad
\begin{array}{r} 6 \\ \times\ 5 \\ \hline \end{array}
\qquad
\begin{array}{r} 5 \\ \times\ 1 \\ \hline \end{array}
$$

$$\begin{array}{r} 6 \\ \times\ 5 \\ \hline \end{array} \qquad \begin{array}{r} 5 \\ \times\ 5 \\ \hline \end{array} \qquad \begin{array}{r} 5 \\ \times\ 7 \\ \hline \end{array} \qquad \begin{array}{r} 4 \\ \times\ 5 \\ \hline \end{array} \qquad \begin{array}{r} 7 \\ \times\ 5 \\ \hline \end{array}$$

$$\begin{array}{r} 4 \\ \times\ 7 \\ \hline \end{array} \qquad \begin{array}{r} 7 \\ \times\ 5 \\ \hline \end{array} \qquad \begin{array}{r} 5 \\ \times\ 6 \\ \hline \end{array} \qquad \begin{array}{r} 5 \\ \times\ 7 \\ \hline \end{array} \qquad \begin{array}{r} 4 \\ \times\ 5 \\ \hline \end{array}$$

$$\begin{array}{r} 5 \\ \times\ 7 \\ \hline \end{array} \qquad \begin{array}{r} 4 \\ \times\ 9 \\ \hline \end{array} \qquad \begin{array}{r} 7 \\ \times\ 5 \\ \hline \end{array} \qquad \begin{array}{r} 5 \\ \times\ 5 \\ \hline \end{array} \qquad \begin{array}{r} 5 \\ \times\ 6 \\ \hline \end{array}$$

$$\begin{array}{r} 5 \\ \times\ 3 \\ \hline \end{array} \qquad \begin{array}{r} 7 \\ \times\ 5 \\ \hline \end{array} \qquad \begin{array}{r} 6 \\ \times\ 5 \\ \hline \end{array} \qquad \begin{array}{r} 3 \\ \times\ 8 \\ \hline \end{array} \qquad \begin{array}{r} 5 \\ \times\ 7 \\ \hline \end{array}$$

$$\begin{array}{r} 5 \\ \times\ 7 \\ \hline \end{array} \qquad \begin{array}{r} 6 \\ \times\ 4 \\ \hline \end{array} \qquad \begin{array}{r} 7 \\ \times\ 5 \\ \hline \end{array} \qquad \begin{array}{r} 5 \\ \times\ 6 \\ \hline \end{array} \qquad \begin{array}{r} 4 \\ \times\ 8 \\ \hline \end{array}$$

$$\begin{array}{r} 6 \\ \times\ 5 \\ \hline \end{array} \qquad \begin{array}{r} 5 \\ \times\ 7 \\ \hline \end{array} \qquad \begin{array}{r} 5 \\ \times\ 5 \\ \hline \end{array} \qquad \begin{array}{r} 7 \\ \times\ 5 \\ \hline \end{array} \qquad \begin{array}{r} 4 \\ \times\ 4 \\ \hline \end{array}$$

Name _____

7 x 5	5 x 5	8 x 5	6 x 5	5 x 8
7 x 4	5 x 8	5 x 7	8 x 5	4 x 6
8 x 5	9 x 4	5 x 8	5 x 5	7 x 5
4 x 4	5 x 8	5 x 7	4 x 8	8 x 5
8 x 5	6 x 5	5 x 8	7 x 5	5 x 4
5 x 7	5 x 8	5 x 5	8 x 5	5 x 6

$$
\begin{array}{r} 8 \\ \times\ 5 \\ \hline \end{array}
\qquad
\begin{array}{r} 5 \\ \times\ 6 \\ \hline \end{array}
\qquad
\begin{array}{r} 9 \\ \times\ 5 \\ \hline \end{array}
\qquad
\begin{array}{r} 7 \\ \times\ 5 \\ \hline \end{array}
\qquad
\begin{array}{r} 5 \\ \times\ 9 \\ \hline \end{array}
$$

$$
\begin{array}{r} 1 \\ \times\ 5 \\ \hline \end{array}
\qquad
\begin{array}{r} 5 \\ \times\ 9 \\ \hline \end{array}
\qquad
\begin{array}{r} 5 \\ \times\ 3 \\ \hline \end{array}
\qquad
\begin{array}{r} 9 \\ \times\ 5 \\ \hline \end{array}
\qquad
\begin{array}{r} 5 \\ \times\ 8 \\ \hline \end{array}
$$

$$
\begin{array}{r} 9 \\ \times\ 5 \\ \hline \end{array}
\qquad
\begin{array}{r} 8 \\ \times\ 5 \\ \hline \end{array}
\qquad
\begin{array}{r} 5 \\ \times\ 9 \\ \hline \end{array}
\qquad
\begin{array}{r} 5 \\ \times\ 5 \\ \hline \end{array}
\qquad
\begin{array}{r} 5 \\ \times\ 7 \\ \hline \end{array}
$$

$$
\begin{array}{r} 2 \\ \times\ 5 \\ \hline \end{array}
\qquad
\begin{array}{r} 5 \\ \times\ 9 \\ \hline \end{array}
\qquad
\begin{array}{r} 6 \\ \times\ 5 \\ \hline \end{array}
\qquad
\begin{array}{r} 5 \\ \times\ 8 \\ \hline \end{array}
\qquad
\begin{array}{r} 9 \\ \times\ 5 \\ \hline \end{array}
$$

$$
\begin{array}{r} 9 \\ \times\ 5 \\ \hline \end{array}
\qquad
\begin{array}{r} 5 \\ \times\ 5 \\ \hline \end{array}
\qquad
\begin{array}{r} 5 \\ \times\ 9 \\ \hline \end{array}
\qquad
\begin{array}{r} 4 \\ \times\ 5 \\ \hline \end{array}
\qquad
\begin{array}{r} 8 \\ \times\ 5 \\ \hline \end{array}
$$

$$
\begin{array}{r} 5 \\ \times\ 8 \\ \hline \end{array}
\qquad
\begin{array}{r} 5 \\ \times\ 9 \\ \hline \end{array}
\qquad
\begin{array}{r} 7 \\ \times\ 5 \\ \hline \end{array}
\qquad
\begin{array}{r} 9 \\ \times\ 5 \\ \hline \end{array}
\qquad
\begin{array}{r} 5 \\ \times\ 6 \\ \hline \end{array}
$$

9 x 5	5 x 6	10 x 5	5 x 8	10 x 5
5 x 5	10 x 5	9 x 5	10 x 5	7 x 5
10 x 5	5 x 7	10 x 5	5 x 5	5 x 9
5 x 4	10 x 5	5 x 9	8 x 5	10 x 5
10 x 5	5 x 3	10 x 5	9 x 5	5 x 7
5 x 9	10 x 5	5 x 8	10 x 5	6 x 5

Name _____

$$\begin{array}{r} 10 \\ \times\ 5 \\ \hline \end{array} \qquad \begin{array}{r} 5 \\ \times\ 3 \\ \hline \end{array} \qquad \begin{array}{r} 5 \\ \times\ 9 \\ \hline \end{array} \qquad \begin{array}{r} 5 \\ \times\ 5 \\ \hline \end{array} \qquad \begin{array}{r} 7 \\ \times\ 5 \\ \hline \end{array}$$

$$\begin{array}{r} 5 \\ \times\ 0 \\ \hline \end{array} \qquad \begin{array}{r} 8 \\ \times\ 5 \\ \hline \end{array} \qquad \begin{array}{r} 5 \\ \times\ 4 \\ \hline \end{array} \qquad \begin{array}{r} 6 \\ \times\ 5 \\ \hline \end{array} \qquad \begin{array}{r} 5 \\ \times\ 2 \\ \hline \end{array}$$

$$\begin{array}{r} 3 \\ \times\ 5 \\ \hline \end{array} \qquad \begin{array}{r} 5 \\ \times\ 7 \\ \hline \end{array} \qquad \begin{array}{r} 10 \\ \times\ 5 \\ \hline \end{array} \qquad \begin{array}{r} 1 \\ \times\ 5 \\ \hline \end{array} \qquad \begin{array}{r} 9 \\ \times\ 5 \\ \hline \end{array}$$

$$\begin{array}{r} 1 \\ \times\ 5 \\ \hline \end{array} \qquad \begin{array}{r} 5 \\ \times\ 5 \\ \hline \end{array} \qquad \begin{array}{r} 5 \\ \times\ 6 \\ \hline \end{array} \qquad \begin{array}{r} 4 \\ \times\ 5 \\ \hline \end{array} \qquad \begin{array}{r} 5 \\ \times\ 8 \\ \hline \end{array}$$

$$\begin{array}{r} 2 \\ \times\ 5 \\ \hline \end{array} \qquad \begin{array}{r} 5 \\ \times\ 9 \\ \hline \end{array} \qquad \begin{array}{r} 0 \\ \times\ 5 \\ \hline \end{array} \qquad \begin{array}{r} 7 \\ \times\ 5 \\ \hline \end{array} \qquad \begin{array}{r} 5 \\ \times\ 3 \\ \hline \end{array}$$

$$\begin{array}{r} 6 \\ \times\ 5 \\ \hline \end{array} \qquad \begin{array}{r} 5 \\ \times\ 4 \\ \hline \end{array} \qquad \begin{array}{r} 8 \\ \times\ 5 \\ \hline \end{array} \qquad \begin{array}{r} 5 \\ \times\ 5 \\ \hline \end{array} \qquad \begin{array}{r} 10 \\ \times\ 5 \\ \hline \end{array}$$

Name _____

3 x 4	10 x 5	2 x 6	3 x 9	5 x 4
4 x 6	2 x 9	3 x 3	6 x 5	9 x 0
5 x 7	3 x 6	4 x 9	1 x 7	5 x 3
4 x 4	3 x 8	10 x 3	9 x 5	8 x 2
8 x 4	4 x 2	5 x 5	7 x 3	10 x 4
2 x 7	5 x 8	10 x 2	4 x 7	2 x 5

44

Answer Key
Level A Multiplication

Page one (Pretest)

10	28	20	40	14
40	21	25	8	32
16	45	30	24	16
15	9	36	18	35
0	30	9	18	24
20	27	12	50	12

Page two (0-Rule)

0	0	0	0	0
0	0	0	0	0
0	0	0	0	0
0	0	0	0	0
0	0	0	0	0
0	0	0	0	0

Page three (1-Rule)

3	9	7	2	5
8	10	0	4	0
0	1	0	3	9
6	0	8	0	7
0	5	10	2	4
7	0	1	8	6

Page four (2x2)

0	10	4	5	4
4	4	0	4	7
4	3	4	0	2
1	4	0	9	4
4	5	4	4	0
8	4	0	4	6

Page five (2x3)

4	7	6	0	6
1	6	0	6	4
6	4	6	4	9
0	6	4	6	6
6	2	6	0	4
4	6	8	6	0

Page six (2x4)

6	0	8	4	8
4	8	3	8	6
8	6	8	0	4
0	8	6	8	8
8	4	8	10	6
6	8	5	8	4

Page seven (2x5)

8	4	10	6	10
4	10	9	10	8
10	8	10	0	6
6	10	8	4	10
10	6	10	1	8
8	10	4	10	6

Page eight (2x6)

10	8	12	0	12
4	12	6	12	10
12	10	12	2	8
4	12	10	4	12
12	6	12	7	10
10	12	8	12	6

Page nine (2x7)

12	6	14	10	14
8	14	4	14	12
14	12	14	0	10
6	14	12	8	14
14	10	14	4	12
12	14	8	14	8

Page ten (2x8)

14	10	16	12	16
12	16	4	16	14
16	14	16	8	12
6	16	14	10	16
16	8	16	12	14
14	16	10	16	8

Page eleven (2x9)

16	14	18	12	18
10	18	6	18	16
18	16	18	8	14
12	18	16	10	18
18	14	18	4	16
16	18	12	18	14

Page twelve (2x10)

18	12	20	6	20
16	20	14	20	18
20	18	20	12	16
8	20	18	10	20
20	16	20	14	18
18	20	14	20	16

Page thirteen (2's test)

0	10	14	4	18
12	16	6	12	10
18	4	8	20	6
14	2	4	0	16
8	12	18	10	2
20	14	6	16	8

Page fourteen (3x2)

20	16	6	18	6
12	6	14	6	20
6	20	6	16	18
14	6	20	10	6
6	18	6	14	20
20	6	16	6	18

Page fifteen (3x3)

6	16	9	14	9
10	6	18	9	6
9	14	9	20	16
8	9	6	18	9
9	12	9	14	6
20	9	16	9	18

Answer Key
Level A Multiplication

Page sixteen (3x4)

9	18	12	14	12
10	12	16	12	9
12	9	12	20	18
14	12	9	12	12
12	16	12	8	9
9	12	18	12	20

Page seventeen (3x5)

12	9	15	18	15
16	15	14	15	12
15	12	15	20	9
18	15	12	6	15
15	12	15	16	12
12	15	9	15	14

Page eighteen (3x6)

15	9	18	12	18
18	18	16	18	15
18	15	18	10	12
9	18	15	20	18
18	12	18	8	15
15	18	9	18	12

Page nineteen (3x7)

18	9	21	12	21
18	21	20	21	18
21	18	21	14	12
9	21	18	16	21
21	12	21	12	18
18	21	18	21	9

Page twenty (3x8)

21	10	24	15	24
4	24	18	24	21
24	21	24	12	18
15	24	21	6	24
24	18	24	8	21
21	24	9	24	15

Page twenty-one (3x9)

24	21	27	12	27
18	27	16	27	24
27	24	27	18	21
9	27	24	18	27
27	21	27	15	24
24	27	18	27	21

Page twenty-two (3x10)

27	21	30	24	30
18	30	15	30	27
30	27	30	14	24
9	30	27	21	30
30	24	30	12	27
27	30	24	30	18

Page twenty-three (3's test)

24	18	30	9	47
3	12	21	6	15
9	27	3	18	0
30	21	0	24	12
15	6	18	27	9
12	24	15	21	30

Page twenty-four (4x2)

30	24	8	27	8
21	8	18	8	30
8	30	8	12	27
15	8	30	24	8
8	27	8	18	30
30	8	24	8	21

Page twenty-five (4x3)

8	24	12	9	12
21	12	18	12	8
12	9	12	24	30
16	12	8	27	12
12	18	12	15	21
8	12	27	12	30

Page twenty-six (4x4)

12	27	16	24	16
21	16	18	16	12
16	12	16	8	27
24	16	30	15	16
16	21	16	18	12
12	16	27	16	24

Page twenty-seven (4x5)

16	18	20	21	20
27	20	14	20	16
20	16	20	24	12
21	20	16	30	20
20	27	20	18	16
16	20	24	20	8

Page twenty-eight (4x6)

20	16	24	21	24
27	24	20	24	20
24	20	24	8	16
24	24	20	30	24
24	16	24	12	20
20	24	16	24	27

Page twenty-nine (4x7)

24	16	28	20	28
18	28	24	28	24
28	24	28	16	20
8	28	24	30	28
28	20	28	12	24
24	28	16	28	27

Page thirty (4x8)

28	24	32	24	32
15	32	16	32	28
32	28	32	20	24
16	32	28	27	32
32	24	32	18	28
28	32	24	32	20